What Could Be Next?
Achieving A Balanced Path for Women Attorneys

Jan Myers Cook, J.D.

978-1-917728-10-2

All rights reserved. 2025 ©Jan Myers Cook

https://www.jancookleads.com/

All intellectual property rights, including copyright, design, and publishing, rest with the author. No part of this book may be reproduced or transmitted in any way, including any written, electronic, recording, or photocopying, without written permission of the author. This book is intended for your personal and professional use.

Published by Orla Kelly Publishing.

"I have great respect for the past. If you don't know where you've come from, you don't know where you're going. I have respect for the past, but I'm a person of the moment. I'm here, and I do my best to be completely centered at the place I'm at, then I go forward to the next place."

Dr. Maya Angelou

Dedication

This book is dedicated to my two loving miracle daughters, Elana and Lea Cook, and especially to my husband, William, who always felt that I had a story to tell—even when I felt that I did not—and who supported me through living the story, and finally, revealing it.

I also dedicate this book to the memory of Jen* (not her real name) for the incredible faith she displayed despite what she experienced during her illness.

Contents

Dedication iv

A Friend's Story Motivates Me vii

Foreword ix

Preface xii

Start NOW to change the path of your life. 1

Chapter 1: There Must Be Something More 3

Chapter 2: Becoming an Attorney - The Early Years 7

Chapter 3: The Need to Pivot 9

Chapter 4: Can You See It? 16

Chapter 5: Discovering Who, What, Where,
  How & When 26

Chapter 6: Following the 7-Step Process
  to your Next Stage of Life 37

Chapter 7: Reflection 39

Chapter 8: Taking the Next Step
  Towards a Fulfilling Life 41

Bonus 44

About The Author 45

References 46

A Friend's Story Motivates Me

I met Jen* when I was in college when my friend introduced her cousin to me. Although Jen and I didn't see each other for several years after college, my friend often shared Jen's stories of success with her family and career. Jen became a black successful businesswoman in the early 1980's for a major United States corporation. About five years ago, Jen introduced me to one of her accomplished adult children who was finishing graduate school in New York. Then, three years ago, Jen was diagnosed unexpectedly with terminal pancreatic cancer. Jen wanted to speak to me while she was enduring her difficult journey through cancer treatment.

Jen felt that I could understand what she was going through because she was aware that I had had my own cancer challenge in my twenties. She knew that I shared a mutual belief in God with her, and she believed that I could encourage her through her treatments. It turned out that we were more compatible than I had realized. I was able to speak to Jen through her arduous journey. As a woman, mother, wife, attorney, counsellor at law, and a survivor, I was equipped both to listen and to understand her. Jen and I agreed to speak by phone regularly, whenever she needed to talk.

Several months into her treatment, Jen shared with me that her daughter wanted her to fill out a guided journal, documenting the significant moments of her life, her upbringing, and the ways these experiences molded her into the woman that she became. Jen was keen on writing her narrative for her children and grandchildren, sharing tales of her early life, her experiences living in various countries, and her career in corporate America. She worked for many years in China and embraced the culture. Years later, after she retired and returned to the United States, she earned a Ph.D. in Chinese Studies.

Sadly, Jen passed away after battling cancer for over a year. She exhibited courageous strength during those final months when I spoke to her by phone during bouts of extreme pain. Although it appeared that she would not finish writing her story, her strength was evident. She was trying to complete the story of her life, but she was not strong enough to do it. I believe that when Jen passed away, she was at peace that she had shared her life with her family. Jen believed that God would continue to support them through their grief at her loss.

I am certain that Jen's story continues to have a profound effect on her family. Throughout her battle with illness, her strength, faith, and determination were clearly visible. Her fierce intelligence, warm heart, and genuine spirituality deeply moved me, and served as a powerful example.

What she showed me when she passed away was that someone's story can have a profound impact on those who read or hear it. Her story demonstrated how a courageous woman overcame the difficulties that she faced in her life's journey. I am grateful that I was able to support Jen, and I know that she felt it. I am hopeful that my life and work will continue to support other women in their journeys.

Foreword

A resilient person is someone who can adapt well to difficult situations and bounce back from them. A persevering person will continue to make efforts to achieve something, even when it's difficult. When both these traits are present in someone, that is a dynamic individual. Add to that person's character, the faithfulness of belief in a God who can do all things, and you will find Jan Myers Cook, my wife! I have been married to Jan for 41 years. I met her in high school 55 years ago. After graduation, she went to Tufts University and then on to law school at Rutgers University. I went on to Drexel University, a five-year Co-op school which afforded me the opportunity to gain real life work experience in the pharmaceutical, analytical, and science testing environments. I went on to the University of Connecticut for my master's degree in microbiology, and then Jan and I married two years later.

I knew Jan was something special (an old cliché, but appropriate). In high school, in our very difficult Mechanic Drawing class, the teacher called us all Mr. and Ms. but referred endearingly to Jan as Jan. She conquered that class and many other difficult ones while still having time to perform in the school's dance troupe. Tufts University was difficult, but Jan graduated with a B.S., *cum laude*, with a double major in Mental Health and English. Jan then moved on to Rutgers University School of Law to obtain her Juris Doctorate.

Jan Myers Cook, J.D.

I started working in the pharmaceutical industry as a microbiologist and eventually fortified my career in a consumer and health product company as a Worldwide Quality Assurance (QA) Director traveling to over 30 different countries developing QA leaders and teams.

Shortly after starting her career in law, Jan developed a cancer – Hodgkin's lymphoma. After a severe year of radiation therapy and chemotherapy, as well as the interruption in her career and new married life, Jan bounced back into a successful government legal career.

As we contemplated having children, she was told that the severity of her cancer treatment impaired her ability to have children. However, being a woman of great faith, when her general practitioner said, *Give it a try, and leave it up to the Lord*, she conceived a healthy baby girl. Four years later, we tried again and conceived another healthy baby girl. Blessed with two miracle babies, Jan continued her legal career and later began a long private practice in elder law. She helped many families, churches, and relatives with their legal affairs in healthcare and estate planning, wills, and financial issues. Jan also served on non-profit boards, gave seminars, and continued to develop her expertise in elder law through continuing legal education courses.

Jan has maneuvered successfully through the legal field as a black woman attorney who overcame personal health issues and combated discriminating male attitudes toward working mothers. She has defined and managed a successful legal and post-legal journey while helping others along the way. Jan has done it all while staying faithful, helpful, loving, and conscientious to her family and friends.

What Could Be Next?

You need to read this work, ponder the questions, and contemplate how Jan's experience can help you with your next step!

~ William Cook

Preface

"What Could Be Next?" is written for the seasoned professional woman, especially the attorney of color, who has worked for many years and feels that something is still missing from her life. She feels like there has not been any time to discover and develop a meaningful relationship with a partner or spouse. If she wants to continue working, but wants to do so on her terms, then this book is for her. She may have decided to leave the law and work in another profession. Or, alternatively, she may want to work in another area of law. A woman of color may want to make a difference in the world while she is still earning an income.

I wrote this book for a woman who is serious about moving into her next stage of life and living it differently. My goal is to help her figure out what could be next in her life.

This book will help her navigate to a more fulfilling life. She has wanted that for years, but she has not had the time to figure out what she wanted, or how to achieve it. I have developed an approach that will help her find what she wants, aligning it with her values and understanding of herself.

I am a black woman who worked as an attorney for nearly four decades in New York City, my hometown. I spent my law career in both the public and private sectors.

Shortly after graduating from law school I began working in civil rights and continued for several years. Still early in my career, I moved to a new job when I faced overcoming a devastating personal challenge.

What Could Be Next?

After overcoming that challenge, I made a shift in my career to work in the field of government contracts. I handled transactions for consulting and professional services for a city agency responsible for working with businesses. I developed astute skills as a dealmaker, negotiating deals that benefited the city, were fair to the contractors, and adhered to lawful procedures without any trace of corrupt practices.

While working on contracts, I was often the only person of color working as an attorney at the executive-level meetings. In one situation, I was directed to meet with the deputy mayor to devise a revamping of the government contracting process. I returned the next day with strategies that identified the legal pitfalls and I designed an operational plan for changing the New York City contracting procedures, especially for small, women-owned and minority, owned businesses.

While working as the Contracts Chief for a governmental housing agency, I was faced with a catastrophe within my first week of a new job. A large public housing building had exploded while it was undergoing a multi-million-dollar renovation. I led a team of attorneys and determined which of the businesses were likely liable based on the terms of the agency's contracts. I identified what needed to be done for residents who were injured or had died. The work with this agency was intense and complicated because it involved housing for thousands of low-income people and transactions that covered vastly different areas of law.

I was frequently challenged by construction contractors during the early weeks after taking the job. I was tested by contractors to see how far they could intimidate me to respond to their issues and give them the result they wanted. In one situation, the general contractor for a company called me on the phone for the first time and cursed at me because he demanded a certain decision regarding a project. I asserted my position, demanding that he speak with me respectfully and established boundaries by yelling back at him. As a woman of color in an executive role, my response to him helped to establish the necessary parameters for my relationships with other contractors, agency staff and managers.

By this stage of my life, I was married with two children, and I had an 11 hour workday. My daily schedule included picking up the kids and dealing with the New York City subway. Added to my hectic schedule were my concerns for my elderly and sick parents. I had become a part of the "sandwich generation," and I had to balance the almost overwhelming needs of our kids and our parents at the same time. I was aware of the challenges families faced with elderly parents since I was experiencing those same challenges.

I made a notable turn to the private sector in the second half of my career. I switched paths from working for the government and I founded an elder law practice. I worked with seniors and their adult children through some of their most challenging financial and health experiences of their lives. I have the unique ability to work with people who need help sorting through daunting lifetime experiences.

After 14 years in private practice, I retired from the law and I reinvented my career through professional courses to become a transformational coach skilled in helping individuals make needed personal and career changes. After completing my certification training, I developed the skills to help individuals figure out their options for their lives. I have the ability, training, and talent to help you discover what blocks your transition to the next stage of career and life.

What Could Be Next?

My attributes are a significant part of why I can help you. I am resilient, curious, and trustworthy. These traits have made the difference in my career with my colleagues and with my clients in my private practice. You can count on my trustworthiness when you want an honest answer as you engage in your new journey to what's next. I've experienced hardships, so I can empathize. Curiosity enables me to inquire about what matters to you, listen, and hear your deepest concerns.

What Could Be Next? is your guide to creating a plan or blueprint for the future. This book will inspire you to explore what you want to achieve and reconnect with your true self as you transition into the next chapter of your life. It encourages you to focus on your passions and the things you truly love doing.

Begin the process to achieve the life you want. You can take the first steps with my simple process whenever you have a moment— on the train, on the bus, in the hair salon, at the nail salon, or your desk over lunch.

Start NOW to change the path of your life

Chapter 1

There Must Be Something More

What are the problems that we face as seasoned women professionals?

Being a professional woman in a high-pressured career is challenging, but being a black woman attorney is immensely challenging. I am writing this book from my perspective as a New York attorney for forty years, but these stifling issues are present in other careers too, such as in the practice of medicine.

The legal profession is demanding, requiring long hours, intense concentration, and unwavering commitment. For a woman attorney of color, especially one over fifty, the emotional toll of your career can be overwhelming. As a woman, you are often faced with unique challenges that impact our mental health, personal relationships, and your sense of fulfillment overall.

You have spent years dedicating yourself to your career. Having sacrificed personal relationships and family time for professional success, you often feel frustrated and exhausted. The relentless focus on your career while sacrificing most of your personal time can make you feel that something crucial is missing from your life.

Work-Life Balance
The struggle to maintain a semblance of work-life balance impacts each professional woman profoundly. Many attorneys experience both emotional and clinical depression, leading some to turn to alcohol abuse and, in extreme cases, suicide.[1,2] The constant stress and pressure can not only affect your mental well-being, but it can also strain your relationship with your spouse or partner. In so many instances, you have not even taken the time to develop and establish relationships with significant others.

Career Progression
Barriers to career progression further compound the emotional stress experienced by women. You often feel undervalued and face systemic challenges that hinder your professional growth, your income, and your access to clients and mentors. You desire a more meaningful and satisfying life, but you are unsure about how to achieve it. You seek clarity on what you want and about what matters to you, and you need guidance to take the leap towards a different path.

You Need to Make a Change
Have you noticed how unhappy and unfulfilled you have felt for many years, but you haven't taken the steps to change your situation? Do you need support and encouragement to help map out a way forward? First, it was the pandemic, and now, the current political climate has intensified your personal desire for change.

These external factors have heightened the stress and have made it clear to you that it is time to make a change in your life or work. You can't avoid the feelings of dissatisfaction; you have spent so many years working, and yet, you still don't have enough time for yourself to do what you love.

No matter how hard it is, you know that you must make a change in your personal life or work.

Imagine just how satisfying your life could be once you figure out what you want to do, and how. What does satisfaction look like to you today? Is it a big house in this country, or *in another country*, or a small house by the beach, or is it late in the morning every day, doing whatever you want? Is it connecting with some special person that cares for you and understands you in a way that no one else does? If these are your dreams, or there are others that you have imagined, let's prepare to make them a reality. Envision the fulfilling life that you are missing.

How Can I Help You?

The purpose of this book is to engage you in discovering who you are as you navigate these next stages of life. I will help you to find your vision and understand and accept that you can attain what has been missing from your life.

Although you have had many successes as a seasoned professional, including status, and a degree of financial prosperity, your goal is still to feel fulfilled. The process described in this book will help you to:

1. Find the vision of what you want in your next stage of life through self-examination.
2. Consider your vision and look at it from different perspectives.
3. Identify your strengths and their application to your vision

4. Clarify the details of you vision by answering the questions in the book
5. Transform your vision into reality by engaging with me in a transformation process of self-discovery.

You have evolved over the years, as well as your life and work. Many people and events have impacted your choices, your core values, and your decisions. Consequently, some of your earlier desires about your career and its impact on your personal life may have changed too, sometimes unintentionally.

I can relate to your scenario. Let us walk through solutions that can help you gain fulfillment during this season of your life. Keep reading!

Chapter 2

Becoming an Attorney - The Early Years

I dreamed of becoming an attorney from early in my childhood. What's amazing is that I achieved an improbable goal. My family was working class. I was born and raised in New York City, and we lived in apartments in Harlem and in The Bronx. My mother worked for the postal service, and my father was a bartender. After many years my father became the part owner of a cocktail lounge. We didn't have much money, but we had enough for essentials such as food, clothes, a place to live, and some extras, but no trips or extravagant purchases.

For years, throughout my childhood, I dreamed of becoming a lawyer, perhaps spurred by television shows such as *Perry Mason*, and the civil rights and war issues which impacted my world and the studies at schools I attended.

Although we had limited money and no connections to make my professional path easier, my mother never ignored my dream of becoming a lawyer. I excelled throughout school; I attended public school until college. I was self-motivated, and my teachers commented on my personal drive. My mother encouraged me and told me that I could be anything I wanted to be if I worked at it. My mother was laid back when it came to me completing my schoolwork, as she did not want to exert too much pressure on me.

On the other hand, my father expected good grades from me, and he tried to support my efforts by providing me with whatever books or equipment—even expensive ones—that would help me to succeed. Sometimes I didn't know how or why I needed those special items, but my father saw that I was bright, and he wanted to give me a chance to be my best. My parents were a model of hard work and determination. I embraced these characteristics as my own, and they helped me to succeed in school and in my career.

My parents supported me financially so that I could attend Tufts University in Massachusetts, and Rutgers Law School in New Jersey. I earned academic scholarships and took out student loans to supplement the payments needed to complete school.

I completed law school at the end of the 1970's. I was hired for my first law job after graduating, and two years later I moved to Albany, New York to work for the New York State governor's commission in a newly developing field of mental health law. The commission was responsible for uncovering physical abuse and fiscal abuse of mentally ill and developmentally disabled patients.

A few years later I got married and returned to New York City. I was looking to move on from mental health law to litigation and I found another job in the public sector. We got married in the spring of 1983, and we moved to a fantastic apartment in New York City with a terrace and a view of Central Park. It was not luxurious, but it was large, safe, and rent stabilized, so we could afford it.

In September 1983, I started my new job working in civil litigation for the Corporation Counsel, the City of New York government attorney's office. I realized quickly that our agency was inundated with work and under-resourced. The salary was much too low for the volume of work that we were expected to complete.

Chapter 3

The Need to Pivot

Almost immediately after I started my new job, the amount of work and the complexity of the work became intense, and the hours were long. I noticed that I had started feeling more tired than I thought I should have, even with the late hours, because I was used to hard work as an attorney. During the first week of work, I arrived home late each night. One night I noticed I had developed a large lump on the side of my neck. It seemed to appear out of nowhere.

Over a period of a month, I went to see my doctor to find out what was wrong. My doctor scheduled weekly follow-up appointments so he could see if the lump on my neck was getting larger, but he didn't order any blood tests to help him with a diagnosis. He suggested that I might have infectious mononucleosis (I did not), preferring to guess rather than test to figure out the problem. He didn't seem to know what was happening to me and I lost all confidence in him.

By the end of the month, I switched to another doctor. He wanted to admit me immediately in the hospital for a week for a series of medical tests since he couldn't diagnose the problem either. I had only been on my new job for four weeks so I told the new doctor *that I couldn't possibly take off any time.* I rationalized that I had no pain, and I had always been healthy, so it never occurred to me that I could be seriously ill. My doctor insisted that I be admitted to the hospital for about a week for tests.

After almost a week of these tests, I was relieved that the early results showed no evidence of disease. Finally, on the last day of my admission, the doctor had conclusive results. He told me, "You have cancer. Hodgkin's Disease, a Hodgkin's Lymphoma. It's a treatable cancer, but there is no operation to remove the cancer and no promise of a cure."

I remember hearing him, but I felt like I was in a cave, lost in darkness in the moments that followed. I thought, "What was this exotic illness that I had never heard of beforehand?" Later I learned that teenagers and young adults were usually the ones afflicted with the condition. I learned that few black patients survived this cancer because it frequently went undiagnosed until the final stages of illness. Many in the late stages of the illness succumbed to it. I was "fortunate" in that I was not in a late stage of the illness.

I had worried about my job, and what I really needed to worry about was my life! That's ironic. I imagined wishing that I was just having an awful nightmare that would pass by. I was twenty-nine years old, and I was just starting out as an attorney and working in litigation, but at that time, my career appeared to be just a disappearing dream.

This was not the way that most of us would expect to begin married life. Where does work leave room for a life? What is the impact of a life-threatening illness on a recent marriage? We were a couple who had to experience a dynamic shift. It was like being absorbed by quicksand and no one was reaching out to retrieve us.

I was young, but I was not invincible, and I was to learn that lesson through cancer treatments. Being sick got my attention.

What Could Be Next?

The experience put everything in focus. Now I had to establish, with clarity, who I was, and what I wanted to do with my life, even if it would be a much shorter life than I had expected.

It was a difficult moment, but I understood that I had to move on and not become immobilized by my condition. I had a husband whom I had married recently that I loved and who believed in me and needed me. I had parents, a brother, and grandparents who were already devastated after they were told about my illness. In the early 1980s, my family probably (and sadly) thought that my cancer was terminal.

The reality of my situation was in front of me. I had to work for the salary and the health insurance so that I would have access to the medical services, drugs, and doctors that were needed to treat me. I had to believe that I would recover.

My husband was amazing to me at a difficult time. He was and still is loving, compassionate, responsible, and supportive. The experience was an ordeal for both of us. He embraced me and my condition, and we worked together to get through the illness. He was the one who broke the scary news to my parents and grandparents. He was often the encouraging voice of hope as we prayed our way through. It was my faith in God that was ultimately my greatest source of strength and the source that I relied on throughout this ordeal.

The law office agreed to allow me to work shorter hours for medical reasons. I was able to return to work part-time, but my doctor suggested that I not share my diagnosis with the job. I knew it was illegal for them to fire me for my illness, but my doctor reminded me that he was aware that some of his patients had been fired from their jobs after they admitted that they had cancer. I knew I didn't have the energy to wrestle with that possibility, so I did as he recommended.

I continued working, and my office switched my caseload to new cases that I felt were boring, routine motion practice, and not stimulating work. I was grateful to have the work though, because I had health insurance, and if I got fired it would have been difficult to get covered by another insurance since I had a pre-existing, catastrophic condition. By the end of a year, I completed my treatment and was able to return to work full time. *My doctors told me that I was in remission!* This was over forty years ago. **It was a traumatic journey that I did not always believe that I would have made it through, but I did.** I relied on my faith as the strengthening part of my journey. I made some of the right choices.

After becoming ill, I felt that I needed to change paths. I realized that I was not feeling fulfilled by my work while representing the city of New York in various civil cases. Furthermore, after I returned to work full-time, I was always tired and stressed and I needed more personal time to manage my life. My doctor told me that it was best to minimize stress in my work.

I had to balance married life, ill parents, and eventually a child and that required that I work in an office where I would have more personal time. I moved into transactions, the field of contracts, negotiations and procurement, and policy - a career for which I was well-suited. I was an Associate Attorney and then I became a Deputy General Counsel, and senior member of the executive staff of a New York City agency responsible for citywide business development and economic development issues. The work was strategic and required that I was engaged in contracts for marketing campaigns to showcase that New York was a great place to do business.

What Could Be Next?

Early in my career I had a catastrophic experience that I could not have imagined. I had to believe that I would recover or at least interpret what I experienced differently so that I could move on to my next stage. I learned to manage my attitude about my health to recover. My hope was not just to accept the changes that were occurring, but to leverage them, and not just by making do.

Many of us have been thrown off-course or redirected by life's challenges. We have been hurt. By age fifty, most of us have been through difficult changes. Our parents or older family members may have died, or we were overcome temporarily by illness. Perhaps there have been some professional goals that we wanted to achieve but we failed. Most of us have had to live and work through depression as we went through these experiences. We can all share how hard it was to move on from those feelings.

Wisdom Gained from Difficult Experiences

So why can I help you? I am keenly aware that many seasoned professional women have gained wisdom over the years and have worked through hardships. You may have even forgotten how you managed to get through some of those obstacles. You may need help in uncovering the emotional barriers that stop you from leading the life you want. I have the tools to help you move past the roadblocks and transition to your next stage of life.

My early career story is one of unlikely expectations realized. What connects you to me is my journey of overcoming the odds despite the devastating obstacles that I faced at the beginning of my professional life. I was delayed in my ability to advance in my career because of a devastating illness, but I still recovered and accomplished my goals. I shared my story with you so that you can see how I managed to experience a fulfilling life despite obstacles. I want to help you to do the same.

How did I manage my challenges and see a way through to my next stage of life? Figuring out how I would make it through this situation was hard, but a necessary part of my story. Although I was diagnosed with cancer, and the illness was a part of my life, I still had dreams. I had to ask myself whether my career was the only source of my future fulfillment. I decided that I wanted to have a successful career, but I wanted a full personal life. I had to **decide** so that I could choose what I wanted most from my life.

Although I was young and at the beginning of my career, I was flexible enough to change my attitude so that I could move forward to my next stage. This was some of the wisdom I learned through my challenging experiences:

(1) I focused on what I wanted out of life and pushed aside negative thoughts against it. I visualized the life that I wanted to live; this was essential to helping me change my negative beliefs.

(2) I developed my ability to adapt and create what I wanted in my life. I needed to look at options that I would have never considered beforehand. I moved into a new practice of law, which was contracts, an area that I never liked. I became creative in developing options for new things. (Many years later after I began training as a transformational coach, I became skilled in helping others delve deeply into areas that they may not have ever considered.)

(3) I understood that I needed to make the best of my life. In this instance, instead of concentrating on loss,

I concentrated on what I was gaining. I still had much to create in my life.

(4) I journaled, wrote stories, watched movies and doodled pictures of the places I had read about, but never visited. (I had dreamed of traveling to unusual destinations, in unlikely places. I could almost see, taste, hear, and touch those places in my mind. It is hard to believe that world travel would become a part of my life eventually.)

(5) I accepted that life is temporary. As a young woman, I did not think about my mortality until I found out that I had cancer. After my diagnosis and remission, I have tried to live a full life and experience my family. I learned to focus less on my career, so that I could experience more of the people who mattered most to me.

(6) I leveraged adversity; I did not just manage it. I had to ask myself what I could do to achieve my best self in my career without giving up my personal life. I felt that I could not just make do. **I needed to rechannel and redirect my actions and create a career with meaning and intentionality.**

These are the life lessons that I began to develop while I endured over a year of intensive cancer treatments and afterwards. They were not easy lessons. It would have been eye-opening if I had a trusted person to help me through understanding and discovering what to do next. I am grateful that I made many of the decisions that were right for me, guided by these life lessons.

Chapter 4

Can You See It?

"Where there is no vision, the people perish...." **Proverbs 29:18a KJV, The Holy Bible**

Are you searching for a meaningful transition to the next stages of your life? ***Can you see it?*** You've worked for years, and you are now at the point where you tell yourself, "Enough!" or "I'm done. I'm sick of this!" You are feeling dissatisfied, so what are you going to do about it?

Do you have a picture in your mind of what you want out of your life? Wouldn't it be amazing, like a weight lifted off your back, if every day you were able to prioritize what you value most? Do you want to make time to rediscover intimacy and relationships that you have not had the time to find and nurture? Imagine energizing your expertise and talents for greater impact for the world and the community!

What if you did not feel guilty because you spent precious time with loved ones? For a change, you did not have to compromise for the time that you did not spend with them. You want more satisfying relationships, meaning and significance, in addition to financial compensation.

This book begins the process to help you take deliberate action to discover how to become both accomplished and fulfilled during your next stage of life. What would it feel like to give yourself permission, prioritizing yourself, but not neglecting those you love or want to love, to achieve more in life?

How do you see the stages of life differently?

All the world's a stage,
And all the men and women merely Players;
They have their exits and their entrances,
And one man in his time plays many parts,
His Acts being seven ages.
At first, the infant,
Mewing and puking in the nurse's arms....
Last scene of all,
That ends this strange
eventful history,
In second childishness and mere oblivion,
Sans teeth, sans eyes, sans
Taste, sans everything.
William Shakespeare[3]

Like in the monologue, are you feeling challenged by the intense changes that are happening through this latter important stage of your life?

Are you retiring, or about to retire, or have you been downsized, missed partnership years ago, have not been paid what you are worth, or not paid equivalently to your male counterparts, or you have not been valued in the workplace? Perhaps you deeply desire to work differently because you have done the same work in your practice of law for years and you want to do something else. Are you managing the challenges of aging parents with illness, raising children through adulthood, or your own personal health issues?

Whatever I thought of these last stages of life when I first read this monologue in middle school, I am acutely aware today that I have aged. Fortunately, I have not yet reached that final stage, "sans [without] everything." The aged Shakespearean image is a challenging one for me. It leads me to ask you, "Can you accomplish new experiences that you desire to have now at this stage of life?" I know that you can if you want to, but you will need to clarify who you are, what you want, visualize it, and take action to achieve it.

Then, you will have a mission to create the vision for your next stage of life. It takes energy to find your solution among competing demands on your time and life. How do you receive what is missing from your life? This book is about seeing what you want in your future so you can have it.

My Blurry Sight Brought My Vision to Life

When I was a very young child before entering kindergarten, doctors covered my left eye with bandages for weeks at a time. Later the doctors covered my stronger eye (the one that I could see better through) with a black eye patch (Pirate style) when I was attending school. The reasoning was that I had a "lazy eye" and by covering the "good eye," the lazy eye would be forced to see better. The patch and the eye covering did not work. I was teased unmercifully at school for how I looked and because I could not see. Sometimes I removed the covering so that I could see better through the right eye (that had the better vision).

Eventually, as an elementary school kid, I started wearing glasses. Kids still teased me because I wore glasses, but at least

I was not the only one who wore them. My poor vision has been a lifelong drag, but not a true disability. I managed with it and barely noticed my vision as an impediment as an adult. I continued to have almost no vision in my left eye and my sight is not corrected with glasses. My vision is somewhat impaired in my right eye too, but my vision is mostly corrected when I wear glasses or contact lenses.

As an adult I realized that I was extremely nearsighted, and I spent much of my adult life trying to see and understand myself, my circumstances, and other people through a cloudy lens. Isn't it ironic that the things that I "see" and feel inside can often bring more clarity than what I can see physically?

Losing My Sight and Regaining It

I have worked and enjoyed life and not paid too much attention to my nearsightedness. It was not until about 2021, during the pandemic, that I realized that my vision was increasingly getting worse in my "good eye." I knew that I was developing cataracts because my doctor had diagnosed it.

I was having trouble seeing people's expressions on Zoom meetings. I could not even put on my make-up in the mirror unless my face was mere inches away from it.

After meeting with my ophthalmologist, he recommended an operation for cataracts to improve my vision. The doctor looked gravely concerned when informing me that, although I needed the operation, the risk of blindness was greater in my case than in most.

"If ***anything went unexpectedly wrong*** during the operation . . ." and, as he spoke, my attention trailed off and I understood that my "good eye" might not recover if something went wrong during the operation, and I could lose sight in my right eye. I would have little or no vision permanently in both eyes.

Realizing the risks, I scheduled the operation anyway. It was very quick, a less than twenty-minute operation. I was treated as an outpatient in a facility where cataracts are removed surgically on a regular basis. The day after the operation, the mesh see-through covering was removed from my right eye. It felt like I had experienced a MIRACLE, but I knew that it was not really a miracle, but the result of technology and my doctor's skill. Not only could I see better, but I also saw colors vividly, with a sharpness and focus that I cannot ever remember experiencing. Many people who have had cataract operations experienced dramatic results like I had.

What Difference Does My Story Make for You?

Why should the story of my eye operation matter to you? Well, seeing differently is a matter of perspective. After the operation, I could see better – my vision through my eyes was enhanced. I started to reflect on how well I had used other types of vision in most of my successful encounters with people in my work and life. *I found that vision is so much more than just seeing with our eyes. Vision is the ability to imagine, design, plan, and evolve into what's next.*

I am quite clear-sighted now, and I can assist you envision your next stage of life. *I can help you become aware of what you have been missing right below the surface.*

After the pandemic, I decided to enter a program to develop skills in helping individuals discover and achieve more of what makes them feel fulfilled. I took courses, read, and engaged with people seeking to reinvent their personal and professional

What Could Be Next?

lives. I envisioned that I had to become the person who could help you to transform your life.

I have mapped out and planned wonderful parts of my life. I have dreamed and desired trips and experiences that I did not know could be achieved, but they were accomplished. I am a spiritual person with a belief system that has supported those dreams. It has allowed me to see and imagine what has happened in my life.

There Are Several Sources of Vision

You can understand vision and sight in ways that have little to do with images received through your eyes. In this book, I will ask you to think deeply and visualize your future possibilities to have a more satisfying career and personal life outside of work.

Consider the **foresight** to predict for yourself what wise actions you should take to determine what kind of future you will experience. Foresight is so important to make changes in your life and achieve what has been missing as you evolve and move forward.

My office assigned a project to me to develop the plan, policy, and procedures for New York's citywide procurement program. I had to start and finish the assignment by the next day because the New York City's Deputy Mayor set the deadline. I knew that if I did not complete the preliminary work, I would fail at my job and must deal with the repercussions from the commissioner, supervisors and the mayor. But, If I could see outside the box and create something unique, it would be an accomplishment that the upper management would have to acknowledge.

The result was my work became the foundation for the city's business enhancement program and resulted in my promotion and significant responsibilities as a citywide advisor for all the agencies run by the mayor throughout New York City. My past work enabled my ability to design a new approach to arcane and dysfunctional systems. I used my foresight to create a successful result for this project.

And what about **hindsight**? Have you experienced some negative experiences and looked back and told yourself that you would probably not do it again? I have.

When I look back in hindsight, I realize that if I had made a different choice, my career might have progressed differently. After returning to my job as an Associate General Counsel after the birth of my first child and maternity leave, I was encouraged to apply for a promotion in the department where I worked. My work was valued, and I was well respected, so my supervisors believed that I would be a successful candidate for the job.

I did not apply for the job because I wanted to spend more time with my baby. I didn't want the longer, extended hours required with the new assignment, and I doubted my ability to do the work. Another attorney took the job, although she was pregnant. The job was time consuming, but doable, and in hindsight, I should have applied and taken the job. The result would have been higher pay and a promotion. Despite my previous decision, I acquired both more money and a promotion a couple of years later. I often wondered, what if? In hindsight, my decision changed the trajectory of my career.

I am **nearsighted,** but not blind. I can see dimly without glasses, but my story of whether I could see or not, contributed to a lack of confidence in my early years. Eventually I learned to understand myself and accept who I am. I realized that I just see things differently, and I learned to cope and manage my circumstances creatively. I accepted my strengths as well as my areas of continuous improvement. My sight was not wonderful, but what I have is intellectual curiosity, analytical ability, and a voice. Not just a loud one, but one that evolved to resonate, modulate, negotiate, advocate, assert, demand, and persuade. My speaking voice became one of my sources of greatest confidence.

Identify Your Strengths

I can change my voice to be compeling, convincing and dramatic, and I have used it in school and the workplace to argue and debate, act in plays and finally as a significant tool in my work as a transactional attorney. As important as my voice is, and as valued as you feel your voice is, unless you "see" its value, you won't use your voice to your advantage. Most of us as attorneys and counsellors at law are confident users of our voices.

As I entered the profession of law after law school, I believed that, as you may have believed, that I could conquer the challenges that I faced as a woman of color in a career that is dominated by those who would not value my voice or my position within the workspace.

Today, why not use your voice and your strengths to create the satisfying life that you desire? Choose a new office to work in; set out to lead an organization or start a business where you have freedom to control your time, income, and the people you choose to work with. You can use your skills to analyze, research, write, and speak in a myriad of circumstances - even in your latter years. If you have the ability and desire to use your talents and skills, you can make a meaningful difference in the world and achieve the fulfillment that you want.

What are your greatest personal strengths? If you have struggled with personal illness or cared for a sick parent or child, you probably display resilience in everything you do. You manage to move forward with all your responsibilities despite the hardships. Your personal attributes help to define who you are. Think about creating a list of the characteristics that other friends and family say you possess and identify how these qualities helped them and you.

Creative Options for Seeing your Vision

What would it feel like to **explore** and **expose** a side of yourself in a creative way that you have not revealed to yourself or anyone else for a long time?

Option 1: What if you were to dramatize your next stage of life? What would you include if you were to write yourself into a play or movie? Can you **visualize** the dramatic action? As your life unfolds in the play that you're writing, what is the storyline? If it were a movie, who would play the main character, the protagonist, and the supporting actors?

Option 2: Drawing or painting your own work of art –

Do you enjoy drawing, painting, or creating with various media, even if it is just for fun?

What If you prefer to draw your next stage instead of writing about it? Imagine your next chapter of life in visual form. We imagine first in our minds and hearts before we draw physical pictures. Draw your image or make a sketch of the plan for what you might build in three-dimensional form.

Later in this book you will review some questions that will help you think deeply and reflect differently on your life.

Can you envision making the crucial steps towards change after working in your current role for many years? You will probably need help in making these decisions; I can help you there.

Take the first step towards a more fulfilling career. Reach out today to explore how I can support you in overcoming the blocks holding you back. Female lawyers like you deserve a trusted partner to help navigate change—let's start your personalised journey together.

Chapter 5

Discovering Who, What, Where, How and When

In this chapter you will have an opportunity to respond to questions that I have presented to help you gain clarity about your future desires for your next stage of life. You can change your life to achieve the satisfaction that you want, but it is not easy without applying a process to help you see things differently. You can start here in this chapter by writing and creating your vision, using the questions below as a starting point.

Journaling can open your thinking. You will delve deeply within yourself to write your story. Rather than writing on blank pages with no direction, I offer queries or prompts for you to start. Create your personal account of the future life that you want—a life of fulfillment.

The questions of who, what, where, how, and when, are questions that journalists sometimes consider when writing a newspaper article. These questions may seem simple, but they may help to provide you with the direction that you need as you make changes. Let me give you two examples of two questions and the results in my life.

What skills can I use in the future?
I decided to make a change in my career after working as an attorney and being in management for most of my career

in the public sector. I entered a field that initially I did not imagine was possible. I hired a career consultant to help me figure out my next job. Eventually, I followed through with her suggestion, which was to change my career from a government contracts attorney to an owner of an elder law practice.

After my decision to change fields, I reviewed my prior skills and knew that I could make a reasonable transition since I had a relevant legal background that would help me. To make the transition, I had to become the attorney founder of the law firm, and I developed the expertise and the confidence to find clients and address their needs. I took (CLE or Continuing Legal Education) classes to prepare for the new legal work. I developed relationships with other attorneys to enhance my skills and visibility in the profession. Eventually, I built a business that delivered the services that my clients needed desperately.

About a year later after starting my firm, my mother-in-law was diagnosed with debilitating progressive multiple sclerosis that required round-the-clock personal care. Because I had training in the legal areas relevant to her health and financial needs, I was able to help her to get the care that she needed, when she needed it. I even had specialized knowledge of the facilities that would provide her with the best care. My new work experience came in very handy in this situation, plus I was available to her and to my teenage kids if needed. My husband and I were able to support my mother-in-law emotionally and physically as she continued to reside in her home that was nearby our house. My decision to make a change in my life was truly a win-win for my whole family.

Where would you like to live or work?
Where you want to be might have a ***reason*** attached to it. The space, or setting you imagine, may help you to achieve the change that you want to make.

What if you choose a new location just because you want to try out something different? For example, you live in the northeastern United States as I did, and you are transplanting yourself to the South, East or West.

I moved prior to retiring to a new location in North Carolina and lived in a single-family house instead of a condominium or apartment for the first time in my life. I finally saw and listened to the birds in my backyard, and the trees waving in the breeze in the backyard. I had a cup of mint tea and my journal to express my gratitude for bringing a vision to fruition that I didn't realize I had. I made many new friends in my new location, and I have found that people meet and socialize in their homes here more often than in my former city. I found the source of some of my best thinking happened in the quiet times in my home during the pandemic.

What if you are choosing to leave the law profession and make a career change that is totally different from what you do today? If you are an attorney who had always worked inside of an office, but you decide to leave law to become a chef, and then work in a kitchen or a restaurant, would this be your new ideal environment?

One example of a story in which the change of location and work made a significant change for one woman's life occurred for my friend's daughter. She was in her early forties when she decided to leave her work as an attorney to become a farmer. She found that she loved the land, the feel of the soil, and she enjoyed watching plants and vegetables grow that she had tended. My friend's daughter found joy in tasting freshly picked, insecticide-free red, juicy, sweet strawberries and fresh vegetables. Farming truly made her heart sing! Her location made all the difference in achieving her dream.

You may find it difficult at first to answer some of the questions in this chapter. This is okay. The goal is for you to see or consider the questions that you may not have thought about previously. You have values, interests, and desires that are unique to you. By answering these questions, you will construct the next stage mentally.

Go to [link] to download a complimentary copy of a bonus workbook with the following questions.

You can also answer in your own journal or notebook.

Answer these four questions first:
1. Do you have burning fears in your mind about what's next? What are those fears?

2. If you were to reinvent your career or personal life right now, how would you measure success in your new venture?

3. Are there specific people who held you back from making the changes that you wanted to make in your personal or professional life? List them.

4. Are there events in your personal or professional life that have held you back from making the changes that you desire? List them.

Then answer the following:

Who?

Who are you? Describe yourself without using titles or labels.

Who do others say that you are?

After you graduated from law school or graduate school, what were your aspirations? Describe what you had expected to achieve after graduation.

Have your values changed from when you first graduated from law school? Values are a person's principles or standards of behavior; one's judgement of what is important in life. (*Values Meaning - Google Search*, n.d.)
They are views like truth, freedom, or justice, but you are not limited by this list of values.

What are your values now? Describe the values that you express in your conversation or behavior during work or personal time with friends.

Could you be coaxed to give up a value or position under the right circumstances (where there is no coercion or force)? If so, what would those circumstances be?

What would cause you to relinquish or change a value?

What Could Be Next?

Have you ever taken a personality assessment? If so, how did the assessment describe your personality? Does the assessment describe who you are now accurately?

Are you happy, depressed, judgmental, thinking, or analytical?

How do people, who you like, describe you to others?

What are your strengths that you will use in your next stage of life?

What aspect of your personality do you feel will hinder or block some of what you want to do in your future? What has held you back from making a change in your life or career?

Can you use your skills and strengths to make your next move?

What?

What are your future personal goals for your life?

What are your future professional goals?

What were your career and personal goals ten years ago? Twenty years ago?

What do you love to do when you are not working? Are there activities that you do or want to do that thrill you, make you happy, or content and satisfied?

What work do you love to do that you might want to do during this next stage?

Do you want to work for someone, own **a** business, become a consultant or an entrepreneur, work part-time, full-time, and/or virtually? Would you advise, counsel, coach, sell a product, or become a member of a board of directors?

What does the new role that you envision mean to you?

In your distant past thoughts, what did you want to do or accomplish in your latter stages of life?

What would you do if you worked as an attorney in another area of law?

Would it be the same work as you currently do, but for different clients?

What could you see yourself doing that brings meaning to you aside from being an attorney?

What kind of work would you perform that would be meaningful to your new clients? Who will be your clients?

Is it solely your clients who would benefit from your work, or do you desire to have a far greater reach nationally, or globally?

What is the level of impact that you desire to make?

What Could Be Next?

What do you want to do that would make you feel fulfilled?

What hidden talents do you have that you have not had time to engage in, but they give you happiness? (Examples are hobbies like singing, drawing, or philanthropic work.) What can you do to transform a hobby that you love into a career?

What will you do with what you have written down?

What's your vision of your next stage? What would you want to do, or have, or spend your time with or for, if money were no option, and you knew that you could not fail? *Can you abandon your fears and create a vision of having everything you want in your life?*

Once you make the changes that you want to make during this next stage of life, what do you believe you will feel and experience that you were missing in your life previously? Describe your feelings.

> *I now invite you to take a breather. This is a good time to reflect. What has answering the above brought up for you?*
>
> *Are you feeling unsure about your next step? If so, let's explore your motivations and options together. Reach out today, and I'll help you gain clarity and confidence in your decision-making process.*

Where?

Is there a place or location that would serve you best that you could accomplish your goal? Would relocation be a better option for your future endeavors?

Do you want to live or work in the same city, state, or country as you live in now? Do you want to stay in the same location for a specific reason? What are the reasons?

If you'd rather live in a different place, where would it be?

Does the new location have a special significance to you? What's the significance?

Do you want to work inside or outside of an office or courtroom?

With vivid detail, imagine and describe your new location as if you are stepping into the space, the place, or the environment right now.

Is your imagined workspace an environment that is open and collaborative so it will permit you to be your most creative self? Or perhaps you are someone who prefers a quiet, secluded, closed-door space to be productive. Is it a quiet, remote setting that will enable you to move freely and to think introspectively?

How?

How do you make changes into another stage of life and career?

What Could Be Next?

How do you avoid the pitfalls of stress and not having enough money as you embark on your journey?

How will you manage your personal life, work, and finances during transition?

If you are thinking about becoming an entrepreneur, how will you provide products or services to your clients? If your personal time is limited, how can you use your professional time without jeopardizing your personal life?

How would you like the story of this stage of life to conclude? What is the climax of your personal story during this stage of transition?

When?

Can you create an imaginary timeline listing the events that are important in your imaginary future?

When will you start your next stage of life and work?

If you don't have a specific date, when do you plan to leave the job or career that you are in and start your next thing?

Is the move or change that you are dreaming about tied to an event (birth of a child, or death of a parent)? When is this triggering event expected to happen? Explain.

By what date will you begin the steps necessary to commence the next stage of your more fulfilled life?

Creating a timeline can be scary, or empowering, or both. One sobering thought is that your timeline shows you that time is limited. Eventually, you will want or need to slow down your work because **you**, your spouse, partner, or family will get older. You will not be able to do as much. *Do what really matters to you **NOW** so that you can feel the satisfaction that comes with experiencing it.*

Chapter 6

Following the 7-Step Process to your Next Stage of Life

I've created a unique program consisting of several structured steps. These steps provide a framework designed to guide you towards a more fulfilling and meaningful life. Why does this approach work? The steps of the process are rooted in the basic aspects of your life with each step functioning independently to help you clarify your goals for the next chapters of your life. They also enable you to gain a deeper understanding of yourself.

- **Reflect on Your Present Self:** Start with **Steps #1-3** to gain clarity on your current values, priorities, and life situation. Begin understanding who you are today.
- **Explore Your Past for Growth:** Use **Step #4** to lay a foundation from your past—not to dwell on it, but to use it as a springboard for future progress.
- **Create Your Vision for the Future: Step #5** invites you to envision the people, places, and things that align with your future aspirations. Start building your dream life now.

- **Transform Your Subconscious Thoughts: Step #6** will help you examine subconscious patterns that may be holding you back leading to a truly transformational experience.
- **Join a Supportive Community:** Connect with other women in the optional **Step #7** through the S.A.L.T. (Seeking Alternatives for Lawyers in Transition) community. Share experiences, gain mentorship, and grow alongside a supportive cohort.

Learn More about S.A.L.T.

Interested in the S.A.L.T. community? Visit https://www.jancookleads.com to connect and find out how this cohort can elevate your personal and professional transformation.

Stay Accountable to Your Goals

Partner with me as your coach who will energize and support you to act consistently with your values and the life you want.

This transformational process is designed to help you progress more swiftly than you would on your own as you transition through life's next stages. Even if some women don't complete all seven steps, they still take meaningful strides toward achieving their goals. Change can be challenging, and many individuals require support to make significant shifts in their lives and careers. You need an ally to help hold you accountable, align your actions with your values, and rediscover your energy to live authentically.

Discover how this transformative process can work for you. Book a short pilot session today to take the first step towards clarity and self-discovery.

Chapter 7

Reflection

As outlined in Chapter 1, this guide has equipped you with a clear and supportive path to discovering what comes next. Across just seven brief but impactful chapters, you have gained a deeper understanding of yourself and a framework to shape the person you aspire to become in the next phase of your life.

This book encourages you to reflect critically on your life—considering whether you're truly fulfilled or if there's something missing. What if you allowed yourself to see situations from a fresh angle? Gaining a different perspective—often by challenging your current viewpoints and reordering your priorities—can open up remarkable possibilities. Dr. Wayne Dyer captures this beautifully when he says, *"If you change the way you look at things, the things you look at change."* You might already have experienced moments where a shift in perspective transforms a situation almost instantly, simply because you've seen it through a new lens.

Chapter 4 invites you to form a creative vision of yourself. By identifying your strengths and acknowledging the moments in life where those qualities led to success, you gain greater clarity and confidence. These reflective exercises remind you that your strengths can serve you in any circumstance, empowering you to take control and thrive, no matter the environment.

The heart of this book lies in Chapter 5, which introduces a plan for designing a balanced, fulfilling path forward. Through carefully-crafted, thought-provoking questions, you were encouraged to dig deep and uncover new insights. These questions were designed to spark curiosity, evoke emotions, and bring back meaningful memories. They also leave room for those significant "what if" moments—encouraging you to dream big and envision creative solutions. This process isn't just about answering questions; it's about igniting your inner drive and desire to take action.

Your responses to these questions mark the beginning of shaping a rewarding, flourishing "next act" in life. With clarity, vision, and your own inner strengths as your compass, you're ready to make meaningful changes and step boldly into your future.

Chapter 8

Taking the Next Step Towards a Fulfilling Life

"What could be next?" is the pivotal question. Only you can identify what is fulfilling to you. By reading this book, you have begun a significant journey in navigating through your next stages of life and work. You have begun to create your future. Even if you can't understand the reasons why you have not accomplished some of the things that you wanted to do, be assured that you have achieved so much in your lifetime already. At this stage, your journey continues.

Essential to your journey is continuing the process with a person that can keep you on track and help you to accomplish your desires to move on to what's next. Through the steps described in this book and by communicating with me in a one-to-one relationship, you can engage in a transformational process that moves you to execute your unique vision more rapidly.

What if you don't respond to the questions in this book as a pivotal step to your evolution? If you are making changes and moving forward towards what you want, then you are still making some progress, but you will achieve the results more slowly. What if you decide *not to make any change*s toward your vision? Then you will likely *remain dissatisfied* with your life's journey.

Not Feeling Regret
I often hear stories of regret from clients, friends, and colleagues. It's natural to reflect on the opportunities we may have missed or the things we had the ability to achieve but didn't. However, why allow regret to take root in a part of your life that you still have control over?

Take a step towards living a more fulfilling and purposeful life. Time is passing, and it won't pause for any of us. Make the choice today to act, to pursue what matters, and to leave regret behind.

Stop waiting—take the first step now. Reach out if you need guidance or share your thoughts with me. Let's make it happen!

Looking for Peace and Purpose
It takes work to dig deeply and to become aware of what you haven't seen or have not been able to do all these years. You have been putting aside feelings and dreams and blocking thoughts of life-altering change for your personal life or work for a long time.

Can you imagine just how satisfying your life could be once you figure out what you want to do, and how to do it? What does satisfaction look like to you today? Is it a big house in this country, or in another country outside of the United States, or is it a small house by the beach, or is it late morning every day doing whatever you want? Do you want to travel? Is it connecting with a significant other in a deep relationship that means something special to you? What if you had time to talk to your kids, spouse, or family so that you understand them in a way no one else can? If these are your dreams, or if there are other dreams that only you could imagine, then picture the fulfilling life that you can still obtain. *You're striving to find peace in the life that you want to live.*

I've provided a blueprint to compel you to move intentionally towards personal fulfillment in the next stages of your life, or work, or both. If you only *think about or imagine change* without making change, then it will not happen.

Your next chapter awaits – start creating it today.

Don't wait any longer to turn your vision into reality. Take the first step towards a fulfilling future by engaging in a one-to-one process designed to fast-track your personal and professional evolution.

You've already started this incredible journey—now is the time to take intentional action.

Act with purpose. Discover your next steps.

Contact me today at https://www.jancookleads.com and begin the transformation towards achieving what you truly desire in life and work.

Bonus

As my way of saying thank you for reading this book, I'd like to invite you to download your complimentary copy of the accompanying workbook. Here you will be given the prompts and space for writing your answers to the key areas covered in this book.

Remember help is at hand if what you have uncovered in this book has revealed some thought provoking insights for you. Reach out to me on jmc@jancookleads.com

About The Author

Jan Myers Cook is an executive coach, speaker, and author passionate about guiding professional women towards achieving balanced, fulfilling lives and careers. With a career spanning years as a government attorney and founder of a private elder law practice, Jan brings both professionalism and compassion to her work.

As President of JM Cook Leadership Consulting, LLC, she offers coaching, workshops, and personal development tools aimed at empowering individuals to overcome challenges and redefine their paths. Jan's credentials include international certification through the John C. Maxwell's Certification Program, where she trained extensively as a coach, speaker, trainer, and teacher.

A native of New York, she holds a B.S. from Tufts University and a J.D. from Rutgers Law School. Outside of her professional pursuits, Jan enjoys *time with her family, arts, travel, connecting with friends, and exploring personal growth opportunities*—all of which inspire her unique and insightful approach to her work.

References

Chapter One
1. Peery, D., Brown, P., & Lots, E. (n.d.). *"Left Out and Left Behind, the hurdles, hassles, and heartaches of achieving Long-Term legal careers for women of color."* American Bar Association.
2. Liebenberg, R. D., & Scharf, S. A. (n.d.). *Why are experienced women lawyers leaving BigLaw? Survey looks for answers and finds big disparities.* ABA Journal. Retrieved January 12, 2025.

Chapter Four
3. Jamieson, M. (1965). *Shakespeare : As you like it.* In E. Arnold eBooks.

www.ingramcontent.com/pod-product-compliance
Lightning Source LLC
Chambersburg PA
CBHW061235070526
44584CB00030B/4131